D1435531

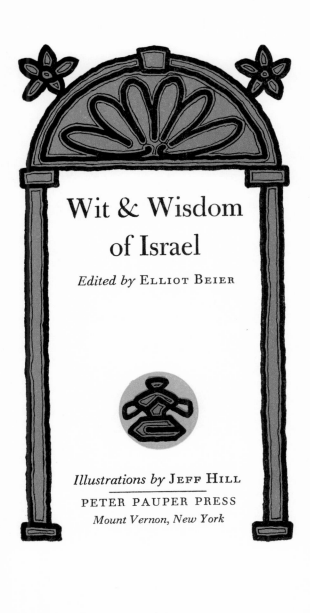

Wit & Wisdom
of Israel

Edited by ELLIOT BEIER

Illustrations by JEFF HILL

PETER PAUPER PRESS

Mount Vernon, New York

Three Blessings

The following blessings reflect the themes of God, Man and Torah — love of God, reverence for life and mankind, and respect for law, tradition and learning. They are the foundation of the wit and wisdom of Israel.

BLESSED art Thou, O Lord our God, King of the Universe, who hast granted us life, sustained us, and brought us to this season.

Blessing for Festivals and Special Occasions

L'Hayyim — to Life!

Toast on Drinking Wine

God make you as Sarah, Rebekah, Rachel and Leah!

Sabbath Blessing over Daughters

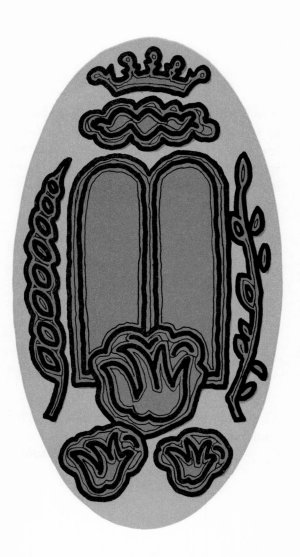

Wit & Wisdom of Israel

A RABBI ordered his sexton to assemble ten men for a Minyan to chant psalms for the recovery of a sick man. When they entered, a friend of the Rabbi complained that one of the men was a notorious thief. "Excellent," said the Rabbi, "when all the Heavenly Gates of Mercy are closed, it requires an expert to open them."

Hasidic Lore

THE first time a thing occurs in nature, it is called a miracle; later it becomes natural, and no attention is paid to it. Let your worship and your service be a fresh miracle every day to you.

Baal Shem Tov

IF I am not for myself, who will be for me? But if I am for myself only, what am I? And if not now, when?

Hillel

5

Rabbi Moses Teitelbaum dreamed that he was in Paradise and saw sages studying the Talmud. "Is this, then, all there is to Paradise?" he asked. He was answered: "Rabbi, you believe the sages are in Paradise, but you are wrong. Paradise is in the sages."

Even for the sake of *one* righteous man the world would have been created, and for the sake of *one* righteous man it will continue.

Talmud

The evil impulse is at first like a passer-by, then like a lodger, and finally like the master of the house.

Talmud

Be more prompt to do what you have not
     promised,
Than to promise what you will not do.

Solomon ibn Gabirol

To every thing there is a season, and a time to every purpose under the heavens.

Ecclesiastes

A MEMBER of his congregation complained to Rabbi Levi Isaac of Berditschev that a teamster was committing sacrilege by saying his morning prayers while oiling the wheels of his wagon. The Rabbi exclaimed: "O Lord, what a holy people is Thine! Even when they oil the wheels of their wagons they pray unto Thee in prayer shawls and phylacteries!"

RABBI Hayyim Habberstam was asked by a member of his congregation: "What does the Rabbi do before praying?" "I pray," was the reply, "that I may be able to pray properly."

THE wise man should be generous in imparting his knowledge to others,
For knowledge is not lessened in the
  giving.

Solomon ibn Gabirol

WHERE there is no bread, there is no education;
If there is no education, there is no bread.

Ethics of The Fathers

RABBI Mendel of Kotzk observed a villager praying most fervently during Yom Kippur services. Knowing that this man was uneducated and could barely read Hebrew, the Rabbi's curiosity was aroused. After services, he questioned the villager. The man confessed: "Rabbi, since I can't read too well, I recited the letters of the alphabet over and over, and beseeched the Almighty to arrange them into the appropriate words of the prayers." Rabbi Mendel said: "Your prayer was more acceptable than mine because you uttered it with the entire devotion of your heart."

ACCUSTOM yourself to awaken at dawn and to rise from your bed at the song of the birds. Do not rise as a sluggard, but with eagerness to serve your Creator.

Rabbenu Asher

A GOOD wife whoso finds,
Far above rubies is her worth;
The heart of her husband trusts in her.
Her children rise up and call her blessed.

Proverbs

A DOUBTER said to Rabbi Joshua ben Hananya: "Where is your God? I cannot see him." Rabbi Joshua stood him in the summer sun, and said, "Look at the sun." "I cannot," answered the man. Rabbi Joshua said, "The sun is but one of the servants of God, and you cannot look at it. Is it not truer that you cannot see God's Presence?"

A MAN is like a letter of the alphabet: to produce a word, it must combine with another.

Benjamin Mandelstamm

THERE are those who gain eternity in a lifetime; others who gain it in one brief hour.

Talmud

THE ideal man has the strength of a male and the compassion of a female.

Zohar

BE a tail of lions,
Not a head of foxes.

Mattathias ben Heresh

THE day consists of twelve hours. During the first three hours, the Holy One, praised be He, is engaged in the study of Torah. During the second three He sits in judgment over the entire world. When He realizes the world is deserving of destruction, He rises from the Throne of Justice to sit on the Throne of Mercy. During the third group of three hours, He provides sustenance for the entire world, from huge beasts to lice. During the fourth, He teaches school children.

Rabbi Judah

IT has been told thee, O man, what is good, And what the Lord doth require of thee: Only to do justly, and to love mercy, and to walk humbly with thy God.

Micah

HE who does not increase knowledge, decreases it.

Hillel

THERE are halls in the heavens above that open but to the voice of song.

Zohar

11

THE wise man does not speak before him who is greater than he in wisdom, and does not break in upon the speech of his fellow; he is not hasty to answer; he questions according to the subject-matter and answers to the point; he speaks upon the first thing first, and upon the last, last; regarding that which he has not understood, he says, I do not understand it, and he acknowledges the truth.

Ethics of The Fathers

I HAVE learned much from my teachers, more from my colleagues, but most of all from my pupils.

Maimonides

RABBI Eleazar said: "Repent one day before your death." Said his pupils: "Does man know when he would die?" He answered: "Then he surely must repent today, lest he die tomorrow."

IF you are in debt, pay your debts before you contribute to charity.

Yehudah he-Hasid

12

THE Emperor asked Rabbi Joshua ben Hananah: "What gives your Sabbath-meal such a delicious aroma and taste?" "We have a spice called Sabbath, which is added to each dish we serve," replied the Rabbi. The Emperor said: "Give me some of this spice." Rabbi Joshua replied: "If you observe the Sabbath, the spice works; but if you do not observe it, the spice does not work."

EVERYONE must have two pockets, so that he can reach into the one or the other, according to his needs. In his right pocket are to be the words: "For my sake was the world created," and in his left: "I am but dust and ashes."

Rabbi Bunam

Do not threaten a child. Either punish or forgive him.

Gemara

WHEN a group of people are sailing in a boat, none of them has a right to bore a hole under his own seat.

Israel Meir ha-Kohen

THE highest degree of charity is to aid a man in want by offering him a gift or a loan, by entering into partnership with him, or by providing work for him, so that he may become self-supporting.

Maimonides

A MAN should so live that at the close of every day he can repeat: "I have not wasted my day."

Zohar

IF you have done your fellow man a little wrong, let it be a great wrong in your eyes and rectify it. If you have done him much good, let it be little in your eyes. If he has done you a little good, let it be great in your eyes. If he has done you a great wrong, let it be little in your eyes.

Rabbi Nathan

HAVE we not all one father?
Has not one God created us?
Why do we deal treacherously every man against his brother,
Profaning the covenant of our fathers?

Malachi

14

ON a fast day, Rabbi Haggai complained to Rabbi Mana that he was very thirsty. Rabbi Mana advised him to take a drink. An hour later, he asked Rabbi Haggai: "How did you fare with your thirst?" The latter answered, "The very moment you permitted me to take a drink, my thirst left me."

A HEATHEN came to Shammai and said: "I will become a convert on the condition you teach me the entire Torah while I stand on one foot." Shammai chased him away with a stick. When he appeared before Hillel with the same request, Hillel said: "Whatever is hateful to you, do not do to your neighbor. That is the entire Torah. The rest is commentary; go and learn it."

WHY was man created on the sixth day, after the creation of all other creatures? So that, should he become overbearing, he can be told: "The gnat was created before you were."

Talmud

THE day is short, the work great, the laborers are laggard, the reward is abundant, and the Master of the house is urgent.

It is not incumbent upon you to complete the work, but neither are you free to abstain from it.

Rabbi Tarfon

A MAN can live without spices, but not without wheat.

Talmud

LOOK not on the flask but on what it contains, for there may be a new flask filled with old wine, and an old flask which contains not even new wine.

Judah Ha-Nasi

IT is customary to make the wedding canopy in the open skies as a sign of blessing, for it is written: "Thus shall thy children be, like the stars of heaven."

Shulhan Aruch

A CARPENTER who has no tools is not a carpenter.

Talmud

THE fate of the world depends upon the conduct of man. If a man is attracted by things of this world and is estranged from his Creator, he is corrupted and he can corrupt the entire world along with him. However, if he controls himself, cleaves to his Creator and makes use of the world only to the degree that it helps him in serving his Creator, he raises himself to a higher level of existence and the world rises with him.

Moses Luzzato

ISRAEL has been compared to the dust: ". . . your descendants shall be like the dust of the earth . . .", and it has been compared to the stars: ". . . I will multiply your descendants as the stars of the heavens. . . ."

When they go down, they go down to the dust of the earth; but when they rise, they rise to the stars.

Talmud

HE who adds to truth decreases it.

Nachman of Bratzlav

WHY was the world created with the letter *Beth* (the first letter of the first word in the Bible, *Bereshith*, "in the beginning")? Just as the shape of the letter *Beth* is closed on three sides and open toward the front, so you do not have permission to be concerned with that which is below or above the earth, nor with what happened before the world came to be. Rather, you should be concerned with what happened since the creation of the world, with what lies before you on earth.

Talmud

A MAN complained to Rabbi Bunam: "The Talmud tells us that when a man runs away from honors, honors run after him. Now I have run away from honors, but honors do not pursue me." Explained the Rabbi: "The reason is that you keep on looking backwards."

GOD waits long, but pays with interest.

GOD gives naught for nothing.

IF THOU intend a thing, God will help thee.

Yiddish Proverbs

19

WHAT words must be used when dancing before the bride? The school of Hillel said: "Say, 'O bride, beautiful and gracious.'" The school of Shammai said: "If she is lame or blind, is one to say 'O bride, beautiful and gracious'? Does it not say in the Torah 'Keep thee far from lying?'" The Hillelites replied: "If someone makes a bad purchase in the market, surely one should commend it. Always make your disposition sympathetic to that of your neighbor."

HE who makes peace in his house, it is as if he made peace in all of Israel. But he who brings jealousy and strife into his house, it is as if he brought them among all Israel.

Simeon ben Gamaliel

WHERE there are no men,
You try to be a man.

Hillel

WHEN Law came into the world, freedom came into the world.

Talmud

BECAUSE a man rising in the morning from his bed is like a new creature in as far as the service of the Creator is concerned, it is incumbent upon him to purify himself and wash his hands out of a vessel, just as the Priest was accustomed to purify his hands daily out of the wash-basin prior to his service in the Temple.

Shulhan Aruch

A KING had a son who had gone astray from his father a journey of a hundred days. His friends said to him: "Return to your father." He said: "I cannot." Then his father sent to say: "Return as far as you can, and I will come to you the rest of the way." So God says: "Return to me and I will return to you."

Talmud

WHO is wise? He who learns from all men.
Who is strong? He who controls his
　　passions.
Who is rich? He who is happy in his lot.
Who is honored? He who honors his
　　fellow men.

Ben Zoma

Rabbi Joseph Caro was accustomed to express a holy intention in words before doing anything. One night he arose for a drink of water, but he could remember no words of holiness to utter. Finally he said: "As I am about to quench my thirst with this water, may it please the Lord to still the thirst of plants and trees." This prayer was accepted and rain which was sorely needed, came down in abundance.

If a man is lying in a ditch, he who would drag him out must come close to him and get a bit dirty. A teacher of public morality is like a broom which can only sweep the dirt out of the house if it becomes somewhat soiled itself.

Baal Shem Tov

Artisans maintain the fabric of the world, and in the handiwork of their craft is their prayer.

Ben Sira

What a man does not work out for himself, he does not have.

Ber of Radeshitz

Two litigants brought their dispute to the Rabbi of Chelm who was widely known for his impartiality. After listening to the plaintiff, the Rabbi said to him: "You are in the right." Then he listened to the defendant and said: "You are in the right." Both litigants departed highly pleased. The Rabbi's wife, who was present, was puzzled. "How is it possible that they should both be in the right?" The Rabbi pondered the question long and deeply, then replied: "You know, you are also in the right."

WHEN I remove from Thee, O God
I die, whilst I live; but when
Clinging to Thee, I live in death.

Judah Halevi

LOVE work, hate mastery, and do not make yourself known to those in political authority.

Shemayah

How good and how pleasant it is for brethren to dwell together.

Psalms

A GOOD angel and a bad angel accompany a man on Friday evening from the synagogue to his house. If, when he comes to his house, the lamp is lit, the table spread, and the couch arranged, the good angel says: "May it be God's will that the next Sabbath be as this one," to which the bad angel, even against his will, says: "Amen." But if it is not so, then the bad angel says: "May it be God's will that thus it may be on the next Sabbath also," and the good angel, against his will, says: "Amen."

Talmud

A FATHER complained to Rabbi Israel ben Eleazar: "My son has forsaken God; what shall I do?" "Love him more than ever," was the Rabbi's reply.

DESPISE no man and hold nothing impossible, for there is no man but has his day and no thing but has its place.

Ben Azzai

BEFORE you can find God,
You must lose yourself.

Baal Shem Tov

A MAN is duty bound to take unto himself a wife in order to fulfill the precept of propagation. This precept becomes obligatory on a man when he reaches the age of eighteen; at any rate he should not pass his twentieth year without taking a wife. Only in the event when he is engaged in the study of the Torah with great diligence, and he has apprehension that marriage may interfere with his studies, he may delay marrying, providing he is not passionate.

Shulhan Aruch

IT is praiseworthy to achieve peace between two men who quarrel. It is even more important to make peace between your body and your spirit, so that materialism does not conquer the spirit.

Jacob Joseph Ha-Kohen

THE higher the truth, the simpler it is.

Abraham Isaac Kook

THE world abides only for the sake of school children.

Judah HaNasi

THE manner of sitting, movements and affairs of a man, when alone in his house, are not the same as when in the presence of a great king. One's manner of talk and boasting when among his own family and friends is likewise not the same as when in the company of a king. In the latter case a man would certainly take precautions that his movements and manner of speech be properly prepared. So much more should a man be cautious when he considers that the great King, the Holy One, blessed be He, whose glory fills the whole earth, always stands near him and observes his doings.

Shulhan Aruch

BE not in a hurry like the almond, first to blossom and last to ripen. Be rather like the mulberry, last to blossom and first to ripen.

Ahikar

BETTER is a dry morsel and quietness therewith, than a house full of feasting with strife.

Yiddish Proverb

27

WHEN Levi Isaac of Berditschev was about to be born, the Satan complained that henceforth he would have no work to do, since the saintly Levi Isaac would be able to induce every Jew to become a righteous man. "Do not worry," replied the Lord. "He is destined to become a Rabbi, and thus he will be busily occupied with congregational affairs."

Baal Shem Tov

BE open-eyed to the great wonders of nature, familiar though they be. Men are more likely to be astonished at the sun's eclipse than at its unfailing rise.

Hayim Luzzatto

TOLD that a certain man had acquired great wealth, Solomon ibn Gabirol asked: "Has he also acquired the days in which to spend it?"

IF you should have a sapling in your hand when they tell you that the Messiah has arrived, first plant the sapling and then go to greet the Messiah.

Johanan ben Zakai

28

Do not study Torah in order to acquire wealth, or to have the honor of being addressed as Rabbi, or to earn a reward in the world to come. All that you do, must have the pure aim of expressing your love for God.

Sifre Ekev

Who is a skilled physician? He who can prevent sickness.

Sefer Hasidim

A poor man who is a relative takes precedence before other poor people, and the poor in one's city take precedence before the poor of another city.

Shulhan Aruch

Even in Paradise, it is not good to be alone.

Yiddish Proverb

If the spirit rule and the body be humbled, man will seek nothing beyond the necessary. He will be satisfied with little and will disdain superfluity.

Maimonides

To what point must one honor his parents? Some merchants wanted to conclude a business transaction with Dama ben Netinah by which he would gain 600,000 gold denarii. But the key to his vault was under the pillow of his sleeping father and he refused to disturb him.

Rav Ulla

How do we know that the Holy One, praised be He, prays? It is written in Isaiah: "I will bring them to My holy mountain and make them rejoice in My house of prayer." What is His prayer? It is "May it be My will that My compassion overcomes My wrath, and that it prevail over My attribute of strict justice."

Rav Tuviah bar Zutra

IF a lecture is not as alluring to the audience as a bride to her groom, you had better not deliver it at all.

Simeon ben Lakish

HE who prepares before the Sabbath can eat on the Sabbath.

Jonathan ben Eleazar

31

ARRANGE your library in fair order, so as to avoid wearying yourself in searching for the book you need. Never refuse to lend books to anyone who has not means to purchase books for himself but only act thus to those who cannot be trusted to return the volumes. Cover the bookcases with rugs of fine quality; and preserve them from dampness and mice; and from all manner of injury, for your books are your good treasure.

Judah ibn Tibbon

As you speak no scandal, so listen to none, for if there were no receivers there would be no bearers of slanderous tales. The reception and credit of slander is as serious an offence as the originating of it.

Eleazar of Mayence

MANY candles can be kindled from one candle without diminishing it.

Talmud

How can man be merciful to others
Who is merciless to himself?

Abraham Hasdai

ONE day the prophet Elijah appeared to Rabbi Baruka in the market place. "Is there anyone among the people here destined to share in the world to come?" asked Rabbi Baruka. Elijah pointed to two men. Rabbi Baruka asked them their occupation. "We are merrymakers," they said. "When we see a man who is downcast, we cheer him up. When we see two people quarreling with one another, we endeavor to make peace between them."

BEHOLD, the days come, saith the Lord God, that I will send a famine in the land, not a famine of bread, nor a thirst for water, but of hearing the words of the Lord.

Amos

WHEN you look through a window you see people, but when you look into a mirror you see yourself. Both are made of glass, but the glass of the mirror is covered with a little silver. No sooner is the silver added than you cease to see others but see only yourself.

Hasidic Lore

EVERY man should make an endeavor to marry a respectable woman from a respectable family. By three traits is Israel characterized: by her modesty, by her mercifulness, and by her practice of charity, and it is improper to form an alliance with one who lacks these distinguishing characteristics.

Shulhan Aruch

WHOEVER does not teach his son a craft is considered as having taught him thievery.

Rabbi Judah

SAID a sage of Chelm: "The rich who have plenty of money buy on credit. The poor who haven't a copper have to pay cash. Isn't it common sense it should be the other way: the rich to pay cash and the poor to get credit? But what if a merchant who gives credit to the poor becomes a poor man himself? Well then, he'll be able to buy on credit."

WHEN a man is at one,
God is one.

Zohar

EACH Jew has within himself an element of the Messiah which he is required to purify and mature. The Messiah will come when Israel has brought him to the perfection of growth and purity within themselves.

Judah Zevi of Stretin

RABBI Nachman Kossover was asked: "Can we think of the Lord when we are engaged in buying and selling?" "Surely," answered the Rabbi. "If we are able to think of business while we are praying, we should be able to think of praying when we are doing business."

WHEN the Egyptian hosts were drowning in the Red Sea, the angels in Heaven were about to break forth in songs of jubilation. But God silenced them with the words: "My creatures are perishing, and ye are ready to sing!"

Talmud

YOUR old men shall dream dreams, your young men shall see visions.

Joel

A ROMAN matron asked Rabbi Jose ben Chalafta: "In six days your God created the world; what has he been doing ever since?" "Arranging marriages," replied Rabbi Jose. The woman scoffed. "Is that all he does? I could do as much myself." "Though it may appear easy in your eyes," said the Rabbi, "yet every marriage means as much to the Holy One, blessed be He, as the dividing of the Red Sea."

IT is forbidden to exact payment from the borrower when it is known that he is unable to pay; even to confront him is prohibited lest he be put to shame.

Shulhan Aruch

EVEN repentance should be attained through joy. We should rejoice so much in God that it will arouse in us regret for having offended Him.

Nachman of Bratzlav

UNLESS the Lord builds the house, those who build it labor in vain.

Psalms

ALEXANDER the Great asked the elders of Israel what a man should do to live. They replied, "Let him kill himself (doing good)." He asked what a man should do to kill himself. They replied, "Let him live (in self-indulgence)."

Talmud

RABBI Noah of Lekivitz was asked: "Why do you not conduct yourself like your father, the late Rabbi?" Replied Rabbi Noah: "I do conduct myself like him. He did not imitate anybody, and I do likewise."

THAT which has been is that which shall be,
And that which has been done is that which shall be done,
And there is nothing new under the sun.

Ecclesiastes

WHEN a person begs for food and clothing, there must be no investigation of his need, for we are told: "When thou seest the naked ... cover him."

Talmud

A FATHER should never favor one son more than the others, for because of a little extra silk which Jacob gave to Joseph, his brothers became jealous, sold him into slavery, and it came about that our ancestors went down into Egypt.

Rav

TEACH your children in youth, and they will not teach you in old age.

For the unlearned, old age is winter; for the learned, it is the season of the harvest.

Hasidic Sayings

POVERTY is no disgrace, but neither is it an honor.

THE poor are always liberal.

IF a poor man eats chicken, either he is sick or the chicken was sick.

Yiddish Proverbs

A NEEDLE'S eye is not too narrow for two lovers, but the whole world is not wide enough for two enemies.

Solomon ibn Gabirol

39

RABBI Menachem Mendel of Rimanov dreamed that he ascended to Heaven and heard an angel pleading with the Lord to grant Israel wealth, saying: "Behold how pious they are in poverty; give them riches and they will be many times as pious." The Rabbi inquired the name of the angel. The reply was: "He is called the Satan." Rabbi Mendel exclaimed: "Leave us in poverty, O Lord. Safeguard us from the favors of the Satan."

WHEN ye reap the harvest of your land, thou shalt not wholly reap the corner of thy field . . . or glean thy vineyard . . . or gather the fallen fruit of the vineyard . . . leave them for the poor and the stranger.

Leviticus

GET for your studies both a teacher and a fellow student.

Joshua of Perahyah

HONOR thy father and thy mother, even as thou honorest God; for all three have been partners in thy creation.

Zohar

As Rabbi Levi Isaac of Berditschev was walking on the street one day, the wife of one of his enemies poured a pail of water over his head. The Rabbi ran to the Synagogue and prayed: "O Lord, do not punish this good woman. She must have done this at the order of her husband, and is therefore to be commended as an obedient wife."

THE well-being of the soul can be obtained only after that of the body has been secured.

Maimonides

A MINOR saint is capable of loving minor sinners. A great saint loves great sinners. The Messiah will see the merit of every Jew.

Baal Shem Tov

Do not forsake an old friend,
For a new one is not equal to him.
A new friend is new wine;
When it grows old, you will enjoy
  drinking it.

Ben Sirach

WHILE Moses was watching the sheep of his father-in-law, a lamb ran away. Moses followed it until it reached some water from which it drank. Moses said: "I did not know you ran away because you were thirsty. Now you must be weary." He picked up the lamb and carried it back. Then God said: "Because thou hast shown pity in leading back one of a flock belonging to a man, thou shalt lead My flock, Israel."

MAN was endowed with two ears and one tongue, that he may listen more than speak.

Abraham Hasdai

IT is forbidden to partake of any food before one has fed his animal. First provide grain for your cattle and then you may eat.

Talmud

EAT and drink below your means, clothe yourself according to your means, and honor your wife and children beyond your means.

Assi

A MAN who goes through life without regard to whether or not he follows a virtuous way is like a blind man who walks along the edge of a river. It is necessary for a man to conduct himself like a merchant who always takes stock of his affairs so that he may not go wrong in his reckoning. He should set aside a special time each day for the practice of self-scrutiny.

Moses Luzzato

WOE to him whom nobody likes, but beware of him whom everybody likes.

ONE who looks for a friend without faults will have none.

LET us be like the lines leading to the central point of the circle, uniting there; let us not be like parallel lines which are always separate.

Hasidic Sayings

ON the Sabbath a man should always walk with an easy and leisurely gait. But to do a good act, a man should always run, even on the Sabbath.

Joshua ben Levi

43

THE Lord does not object even if a man misunderstands what he learns, provided he only strives to understand out of his love for learning. It is like a father whose beloved child petitions him in stumbling words, yet the father takes delight in hearing him.

Baal Shem Tov

To obtain a livelihood from a man is often like obtaining honey from a bee: it is accompanied by a sting.

Naftali of Ropshitz

A SMALL coin before the eyes will hide the biggest mountain.

Nachman of Bratzlav

A POTTER does not venture to test a defective earthen flask by striking it! One such blow might shatter it. But he does not hesitate to so test a flask that has been properly hardened. No matter how often he strikes it, it does not crack. So, the Holy One, blessed is He, tests the righteous and not the wicked.

Talmud

SINCE it is a requirement from God that the body of man be healthy and perfect, because it is impossible for a man, when ill, to comprehend the knowledge concerning his Creator, it is therefore necessary for a man to shun things that tend to injure his body, and to acquire habits that make the body healthy and sound.

Shulhan Aruch

A LITTLE light dispels much darkness.

Issachar Eilenburg

THE Lord clothes Himself with the pride which good people cast off.

Judah Zevi of Stretin

WHATSOEVER thy hand finds to do, do it with all thy might.

Ecclesiastes

OFTENTIMES apparent weakness denotes strength that is to come. At the moment of birth, no living creature is as weak and helpless as man, yet man grows up to be master of all life.

Phineas Shapiro

HE whose wisdom exceeds his words is like a tree whose branches are many, but whose roots are few; and the wind comes and plucks it up and overturns it upon its face. But he whose works exceed his wisdom is like a tree whose branches are few, but whose roots are many; even if all the winds in the world come and blow upon it, it cannot be stirred from its place.

Eleazar ben Azaryah

THE purpose of man's life is not happiness, but worthiness.

Felix Adler

GOD created the world with only one single man, Adam, to teach that, if any man has caused a single soul to perish, it is as though he had caused a whole world to perish. And if any man saves alive a single soul, it is as though he had saved a whole world.

Talmud

FAR more than Israel has kept the Sabbath, it is the Sabbath that has kept Israel.

Achad Ha'am

WHEN you eat and take pleasure in the taste and sweetness of the food, bear in mind that it is the Lord who has placed in the food its taste and sweetness. You will, then, truly serve Him by your eating.

Baal Shem Tov

IF a man does not do good in this world, he cannot put his trust in the work of his father. No man will eat in the time to come of his father's works, but only of his own.

Talmud

THE more valuable a thing, the more effort it demands.

Saadia Gaon

BEFORE a man marries, his love goes to his parents; after he marries, his love goes to his wife.

Rabbi Eleazar

BRICKS are fallen, but we will build with hewn stone; sycamores are cut down, but cedars will we put in their place.

Isaiah

RABBI Moses Leib was late for the Kol Nidre service one Yom Kippur Eve, the most solemn service of the year. Some members of the congregation went in search of him. Nearby they heard his voice singing a lullaby. It was the home of a widow, and they saw him lulling a little child to sleep. The mother had left the infant to attend the Synagogue. It had awakened and cried as the Rabbi passed by, and he had sought to comfort the child.

IF a man intends to commit a sin, God does not reckon it to him until he has done it. But if he intends to fulfill a commandment, then, although he has had no opportunity to do it, God writes it down to him at once as if he had done it.

Midrash

THERE is something higher than modernity and that is eternity.

Solomon Schecter

LOVE binds to faults,
Hatred to virtues.

Moses ibn Ezra

MARK well three things and you will not fall into the clutches of sin: know whence you came, where you are going and before whom you are destined to give an account and reckoning. Whence you came: from a putrid drop. Where you are going: to a place of dust, worm and maggot. And before whom you are destined to give an account and reckoning: before the King of Kings, the Holy One, Blessed is He.

Akabya ben Mahalel

A MAN should eat slowly and with etiquette even if alone at the table.

Nachman of Bratzlav

HE who brings up the child is to be called its father, not he who gave him birth.

Midrash

A MAN came to Raba and said: "The prefect of my town has ordered me to kill a man, or I will be put to death." Raba replied: "Let him kill you; do not commit murder. Why should you think that your blood is redder than his? Perhaps his is redder than yours."

RABBI Akiba risked his life to study and teach Torah, despite a Roman decree forbidding this. He told a parable: "A fox was walking along the bank of a stream and saw some fishes fleeing the nets of men. The fox said: 'Come up on dry land and dwell together with me and you will be safe.' The fishes replied: 'You are not the cleverest of animals, but a fool! For if we are afraid in the place which is our life-element, how much more so in a place which is our death-element.'" "So it is with us," continued Akiba. "If we are in danger when we sit and study Torah which is our life-element, how much more so if we neglect it."

TRUTH is the seal of God.

Talmud

TREES and plants and flowers have language, feeling, and prayer of their own.

Baal Shem Tov

ONLY the lesson which is enjoyed can be learned well.

Talmud

WHEN Rosh Hashonah, the Jewish New Year, fell on a Sabbath, Rabbi Levi Isaac of Berditschev exclaimed: "O Lord, thou forbiddest us to write on the Sabbath except in order to save life. Write us down, then, for life for the coming year, as otherwise even Thou mayest not write on the Sabbath."

EVERY man has three names: one his father and mother gave him, one others call him, and one he acquires himself.

Ecclesiastes

IF you drop gold and books, pick up first the books and then the gold.

Sefer Hasidim

GREAT is work, and each craftsman should walk about with the implements of his calling, and be proud of them. Thus the weaver should appear with a shuttle in his hand, the dyer with wool in his arms, and the scribe with his pen behind his ear. Even God speaks about His work of creation; how much more should man.

Eleazar ben Azariah

IT is best to eat sparingly. Thereby a man tends to lengthen his life. We find among animals and reptiles that those which eat the least, live the longest.

Phineas Shapiro

WHAT is meant by the phrase "May the Lord bless thee and watch over thee?" The meaning is: "May He bless thee with sons and may He watch over thy daughters."

Midrash

THERE are four types of students: the sponge, who absorbs all; the funnel, who lets it in one end and out the other; the strainer, who lets out the wine and retains the dregs; and the sieve, who lets out the coarse and keeps the fine flour.

Mishna

WHERE there is no vision, the people perish.

Yiddish Proverb

NATURE is saturated with melody; Heaven and earth are full of song.

Nachman of Bratzlav

GOD bade Abraham offer his son as a sacrifice, and an angel stopped him. This teaches that none but God can command us to destroy a life, but a mere angel suffices to have us save one, even if it contravenes a divine command.

Mendel of Kosov

HE who learns in order to teach will be able both to learn and teach. But he who learns in order to practice will be able to learn, to teach, and to practice.

Rabbi Ishmael

REMEMBER famine in time of fullness, and poverty and want in the days of wealth.

Ben Sira

HE who is ashamed to ask will diminish in wisdom among men.

Moses ibn Ezra

THE shopkeeper must wipe his measures twice a week, his weights once a week, and his scales after every weighing.

Talmud

WHITHER shall I go from Thy spirit? Or whither shall I flee from Thy presence? If I ascend up into heaven, Thou art there; if I make my bed in the netherworld, behold, Thou art there. If I take the wings of the morning, and dwell in the uttermost parts of the sea, even there would Thy hand lead me, and Thy right hand would hold me.

Psalms

"YOU know," said the school teacher of Chelm to his wife one day: "If I were the Czar, I would be richer than the Czar. I would do a little teaching on the side."

IF a Jew breaks a leg, he should say: "Praised be God that I did not break both legs." If he breaks both legs, he should say: "Praised be God that I did not break my neck."

Yiddish Proverb

IT is unnecessary to erect monuments to the pious; their deeds are their memorials.

Simeon ben Gamaliel

AT the time of a man's departure from this world, there are three who plead for him: his family, his money, and his good deeds. The first two are not deemed to be valid credentials of personal worth, but a man's good deeds precede him and prepare for him the road to eternity.

Rav Eleazar

WHEN a person becomes dissatisfied with his business or profession, it is a sure sign that he is not conducting it honestly.

Elimelech of Lizensk

WHEN you have gathered in the fruits of the land, you shall keep the feast of the Lord.

Leviticus

TEN enemies cannot do a man the harm that he does to himself.

FRIENDS are needed both for joy and for sorrow.

GIVE your ear to all, your hand to your friends, but your lips only to your wife.

Yiddish Proverbs

ABBA JOSEPH, though a Rabbi, was a builder's laborer. While at his work one day he was approached by a man who wanted to engage in a religious discussion. The Rabbi refused. "I am a day-laborer and cannot leave my work. Say quickly what you would and go."

IT is wrong to suppress the views of an opponent. It is more fitting to ponder their meaning.

Judah Lowe

HELP us to see that no work truly prospers unless it bring blessing to other lives, and no gain truly enriches if it add not to the happiness of others. Grant that we may never seek to dispossess others of what they have planted, nor build our joy on the misfortune of our fellowmen. Help us so to live that when we shall have gathered our final harvest, many shall rise up and call us blessed.

Union Prayerbook

THE home is the first line of defense.

Henrietta Szold

LET every person, in every generation, think of himself as a former slave, freed from bondage in Egypt.

Haggadah

THY friend has a friend, and thy friend's friend has a friend: be discreet.

Talmud

To accept a public office for personal profit is adultery.

Talmud

LET your neighbor's money be as precious to you as your own.

Rabbi Yosé

A GOOD name is rather to be chosen than great riches.

Proverbs

WHO acts nobly, him will I account noble.

Susskind of Trimberg

LIFE is not a matter of extent,
But of content.

Stephen S. Wise

WHEN a person is born, all his dear ones rejoice. When he dies, they all weep. It should not be so. When a person is born, there is as yet no reason for rejoicing over him, because one knows not what kind of a person he will be by reason of his conduct, whether righteous or wicked, good or evil. When he dies there is cause for rejoicing if he departs with a good name and departs this life in peace.

Talmud

THE END